Triumph Out of Tragedy

By: Janet Heismann

For Whitney Hammond, you are my best friend and we have overcome so much together. I couldn't have written this book with out your help and support.

I want to thank Linda and Doug Keys; you have been a part of my life for 14 years and have watched me blossom into the woman I am today. If you hadn't have been the angel to come into my life when it fell apart at the young age of 9 and guided me to my path I'm on today, I don't think I would be where I am today. You were my caseworker, but also my mom, sister, friend, and protector when no one else was. Yes it was your job, but you went above and beyond for me long after your "job" was over. To my family, I know I have not been a part of your life forever, but I am thankful for the relationships and memories we have shared since then. To my rugby coach, Josh Collins, you have helped make me the Christian I am today. If you hadn't have stressed Bible study so much to us at practice, I would have wasted that much more time away from God. I said no to you for months, but you kept asking and eventually I said yes. I also want to thank my rugby team; Adam Skelton, you baptized me and have been a great Christian brother; Joe Pleen for the inspiration and title for my book; all of the workers at ETV in Austin, Texas; the wonderful Pal Coordinator Tom Elison; the people of ASU who inspired me – Clint Havins, Michelle Adams, Jennifer Johnson, Lindsay

Boynton and 2010-2011 UCPC Board; PaulAnn Baptist Church. I want to thank, Aimee. The entire time I was writing this book, you were there supporting me through one of the toughest times in my adult life. You were the friend who stepped in and proved to me what a true friend really is. I will never forget that type of love and support. Last, but definitely not least, I want to thank Jesus Christ my savior.

Chapter 1-Introduction

Jeremiah 29:11

For I know the plans I have for you," declares the LORD, *"plans to prosper you and not to harm you, plans to give you hope and a future."*

My name is Janet Heismann, and this is the story of my life. I have gone through things that most people would not be able to go through and overcome. Some days I ask myself, 'how am I still alive? How did I make it this far?' I was able to graduate high school with honors, but I also earned not just a bachelor's degree, but also a master's degree after being told that I would not finish college, let alone graduate high school with honors.

People labeled me from the very beginning and have tried to set me up for failure my whole life. But what they didn't know is that God has a plan – He was orchestrating things in my life for a purpose, some of which took me 20 years to realize. Going from being taken away from my family at a very young age in life to living in and out of the foster care system many times, being adopted twice, living with "Godly men" who were supposed to be my father figures, but turned out to physically and sexually abuse me and being emotionally and sexually abused by my own brother. God had a plan for it all and gave me a story to tell. I fully believe that it's not just my story, but also God's glory. As you read through these pages, I hope you see past stories of abuse, hurt, and neglect; but instead see glimpses of God's love, mercy, grace, forgiveness, restoration and His redemption.

Chapter 2-First Adoption

Romans 8:14-16

For all who are led by the Spirit of God are children of God. So you have not received a spirit that makes you fearful slaves. Instead, you received God's Spirit when he adopted you as his own children. Now we call him, "Abba, Father." For his Spirit joins with our spirit to affirm that we are God's children.

It was very dark, but there were many people all staring and fussing over me on the night I made my entrance into this big world. At 12:05 am on October 14, 1987, my life began. What's ironic is, I don't remember the first few years of my life, but as it turns out, those are the only years of my life that can be deemed as "normal."

At a very young age I was introduced into a system that was going to have an effect on my life and determine where I went to college. What system is that, you're wondering? The Foster Care system of Oklahoma.

When I was five years old, I remember meeting my soon-to-be adopted parents. I didn't want to meet them, but my brother did, so I agreed to go. The family was the Harpers (names changed for privacy). Andy was a war veteran and was in his late 40s/early 50s. Jasmine was in her late 30s/early 40s. When we arrived at the meeting place, there was food provided, which won my brother Collin over instantly. If you serve big foot pepperoni with Coke, then you have him wrapped around your finger. They say a way to a man's heart is through his stomach, and this was very much the truth in this case. As for me, however, I couldn't have cared less. I was very timid and shy (somehow that didn't carry with me once I got older). I stayed on my caseworker's lap the entire time, sucking my thumb and burying my head in his shoulder. I am not sure what it was, but something kept telling me not to go with them or to like them.

On the way back to the shelter, we talked about what we thought about the Harpers. Collin went on and on about them. I, on the other hand, said that I didn't like them, nor did I want to go and live with them. Collin told me that was where he wanted to go, and I could either go with him or go with another family. I was only five and didn't want to be separated from my only family that I had contact with, so a few weeks later, we were adopted. Afterwards we went out to eat and to celebrate. Once we got home, there was a cake and some gifts. It was pretty cool because this was new to Collin and I. I remember that when we were in the courtroom, the judge asked me if I new what adoption meant. I said 'yes, it's when a family takes care of kids who don't have any family and we take their name and become a part of their family.'

Collin and I moved to Elk City, Okla. where we lived for about a year or so. During this time in Elk City, I got to attend my first school as a part of a "real" family. It was here that I was introduced to basketball and brownies (girl scouts). I don't remember much about this time other than this is the time that Collin and I found out the reason I did not want to move with them.

The first thing I ever remember doing that was wrong was stealing bubble gum from the Wal-Mart checkout line. (Although the cashier saw everything happen and I didn't actually get to steal it). The punishment I got from that would set the tone for how my childhood would go. Not only did I get a stern talking to right then and there, but I also got spankings (more like child abuse) when I got home. I was told to go to my room, put my hands on my dresser and pull down my pants. I was then beaten 20 times with a board. Needless to say, my bottom was black and blue with bruises for a week and it hurt to sit or lay down on my back.

Do I think I deserved spankings? Of course I did, but not to that extent. This marked just the first of many that happened over the next three years or so. Ever so often, Collin would run away. One particular night it was very stormy outside. We lived in a singlewide trailer across the street from the church Andy was pastoring. I had done something that I wasn't supposed to. Although I don't recall exactly what it was, what I do remember is hearing the rain very distinctly, almost like it was coming from inside the house. I was told before I went to bed to stay in my room until morning – I was being grounded, so I decided I wanted to just go to bed. At some point I woke up to hearing the rain noise and my nose was running – or so I thought. In reality I was having one of the worst nosebleeds I had ever had, and my pillow was soaked. My nightgown was covered in blood. I kept wiping my nose, but it just kept coming. (At this time I still hadn't figured out it was blood). Finally I got up to turn on the light and try to figure out what was going on, but I had to do so very quickly since I wasn't supposed to be out of my bed. Once I found it was blood, I called for Jasmine to come help me. While she was helping me, Andy came home from the church and started yelling as soon as he walked in the door about why I was out of bed and my light was on. He didn't touch me, but he yelled at me in a way that made me crawl into my own body further than I have gone before. From that moment on, I decided I would do my best to be the best kid around. Shortly after the yelling stopped, we realized that the rain noise was so loud for everything to be shut. After many minutes went by searching the house for the problem, it was noticed that my brother was missing. He had crawled out of his bedroom window and went to the Wal-Mart playground. Collin was not found until the next day. Soon after that episode we all moved to Texas because Andy got job relocation as a preacher in Brady, Texas.

  The next few years were just like the previous year or so in Oklahoma. Collin still ran away and was always causing trouble. I remember at one point being moved to the garage room. There was an added on room to the back of our carport that also housed the washer and dryer as well as two deep freezers. Due to Collin's frequent runaways, our parents decided to switch us and put me outside and Collin inside. There were many nights I remember going to bed with nothing to eat. Finally one day I got smart and started to look in the freezer to see what I could possibly eat. I ate through about a half bag of dog food and three bags of frozen rolls, corn tortillas and probably three loaves of bread over a course of about a few months. Nothing really sticks out in my mind about my time living in Brady other than April of 1998. I was barely 11 years old. For a few months now my brother was fondling me. He would sneak into my room at night and tell me he wanted to love on me. I was very clueless as to what he was really doing. I was very naive. I distinctly remember one night he came in with a Ziploc bag. I was confused why he had a bag, but I soon realized what he was going to try and do. I got really scared and told him no many times. Collin finally gave up that tactic and instead decided he wanted to have anal sex. At this point I still did not know what sex was or wasn't supposed to be. I would try to tell my parents multiple times what was going on, but they would just sort of slap Collin on the hand and say don't do that to her. They never really got him to stop.

Little did I know that my life was about to change in the timeframe of one week. It was a very warm Sunday afternoon and was the year anniversary of my grandmother passing. I wanted so desperately to go out to the grave and just talk with her. She was my favorite person, and I loved and missed her dearly. I remember asking if I could be driven out there and was told no. I went out to my room and started to sob. Andy was in the carport working on something and Collin was playing basketball in the driveway. Andy said, 'if you're going to cry, shut the door. I don't want to hear you.' I replied, 'fine then!' and slammed the bedroom door. I went to my bed and the next thing I knew, Andy was in my room lunging at me. My bed was against a wall that had a window about the middle of my bed. I was practically sitting against the window trying to get away. What happened next is still engraved in my head just like it happened yesterday, even though over 15 years have passed since this incident.

Andy grabbed my neck and dug his nails into me with his left hand and started slapping my face with his right hand. Not only did he get my face but he also got my upper arms. At some point during all of this his wedding ring flew off. Andy grabbed my by the feet pulled me off the bed onto the floor. He picked up my bed and slammed it down with it landing on my feet. He then got his ring, put my bed back and grabbed me. Somehow I ended up back on the bed and he was hitting me on my thighs. During all of this, Collin stood at the window of my screen door and watched it all happen. Jasmine came in at some point and stood there watching, not saying anything. Andy was screaming and I was bawling even harder now. I don't remember what he was saying. I just remember thinking I was not going to make it out alive. After Andy was done he and Jasmine left my room. Collin came back a few minutes later told me to come to the door. He looked me in the face and said to do whatever they told me to next and that he would take care of everything. That night I didn't get anything to eat, nor did I want to, I was not in a place to want to eat. I could barely wear clothes – my body was in distress and I was in a lot of pain, not to mention shock. Jasmine came in that night and told me that I would still be going to school the next day. I was to wear sweatpants and a sweatshirt to school all week. If anyone asked why (this was the middle of April in the middle of Texas), I was to say I was chasing Collin in the back yard along the creek and fell on a log and that's how I got all scrapped up. Not once did I ever get an apology out of either of them.

That week at school was one where I was not really with it and paying attention in class. Every morning, I would go to the nurse and tell her I needed to be doctored. She would ask me what happened and I would tell her the rehearsed version and she would just do what she needed so I could get back to class. I went home Monday and asked Collin what he was doing to get us out of this mess. By Wednesday I was called into the principal's office. I walked in and there were policeman, CPS workers and photographers. I had to give a statement about what really happened and then I was asked if I wanted to go home that night and pack a bag or just go to a safety home. I choose not to even go home and get a bag. My counselor at school saved my life and I didn't get the chance to tell her that until about two years later. I will never forget what one of my teachers told me once they found out the truth. She said that since I back-talked I got what I deserve. Should I have gotten in trouble for that? Yes, but should I have been beaten for it? NEVER. The only thing I did wrong was not tell the truth to the nurse when she first asked me. I wish I could say that was the worst day of my life and that things only looked up from here. But shortly after that, things only managed to get worse.

Chapter 3-Foster Care in Texas

Galatians 4:4-6

But when the right time came, God sent his Son, born of a woman, subject to the law. God sent him to buy freedom for us who were slaves to the law, so that he could adopt us as his very own children. And because we are his children, God has sent the Spirit of his Son into our hearts, prompting us to call out, "Abba, Father."

Not long after I left my adoptive family we were moved to a shelter in a town about 90 miles away. We stayed there for two days and then we moved in with a family for my first of many stops before I graduated college. It was here with this family that my life got worse before it got better. Collin and I were both together, living with a family out on a ranch in the middle of nowhere Texas.

Collin was able to continue doing what he wanted to me now; there was no one around most of the property to keep eyes on him all the time. I had previously mentioned to my adoptive parents that Collin was touching me in my private areas. They just slapped his hands and said 'do not do that again.' But that did not stop Collin. Only this time, there were two other children in the home he could mess with as well. I thought he was just messing with me until one night my foster brother (who was the same age as me) was in the room as well. Collin made me and him do things to each other while he sat there and watched us. It was the worst feeling in my entire life. I still was not completely sure of what I was doing or what was going on. This type of thing went on for a few months. Finally one hot summer day, my foster mom came in while we were playing a board game and Collin was on his way to church camp. She asked us how the 4-year-old knew the word weenie. We both looked at each other and knew this was our way out. We sat our foster mom down and told her everything. She then called the police and my caseworker. That night I sat in front of my caseworker and a video camera and told what had happened to me. Collin was sent to juvenile detention for seven years.

I was taken back the shelter we stayed at prior to going to this foster home. I was there for about two months. When August of 1998 rolled around, we found a group home I could move into. I was the youngest girl of about 12 living in this house. I lived here during 5th grade. I enjoyed it and learned a lot about myself, but I felt more isolated from "normal kids" than I have ever in my life. It was during this time that I really wanted to be adopted again, but things were not looking like that was going to be an option so I made the best of that situation. I grew really close with two of the ladies that worked there. I would go on special visits on the weekends to spend time away from the group home.

At the end of 5th grade, I moved to my last foster home I would ever be in. It was a bittersweet time in my life. I told this family that if a hand was ever laid on me then I would see to it that I would be removed. Dean and Peggy gave it a good run. Over the years that I spent with them, I was eternally grateful for a few great things that they did do right for me. The first one was that they introduced me to Christ. I grew to love God and asked Him to be my savior. I was baptized on February 14, 2000. Over the next couple years, I lived a Christian life, going through the motions but not really feeling it in my heart. It would not be until my senior year in college (9 years later) when I would come to truly love the Lord.

Dean and Peggy also found my brother and took me to see him my junior year in high school. It was awesome to be able to reconnect with him and to meet his family. In September of this year (2004) I received a letter from my brother that helped me in ways nothing else really could. Most of my life people told me that I got what I deserved and it was all my fault. Some of the things that happened to me, I could agree with if I didn't know any better. However, I never believed what my brother did to me was my fault.

Dear Janet,

Sorry I haven't talked to you in so long!!! But life has been really busy...how are you?? How is life treating you, good I hope? This letter is not an easy letter for me and probably won't be too easy for you but there are some things I really need to say to you.... I have done many things that have left scars on peoples lived and yours is of them. Janet I did many things to you that were not right, never have been right, and never will be right....Janet I really think and believe from the bottom of my heart that I owe you an apology...by doing what I did I lost the person that I loved the most and the only family that I have. Janet you are a wonderful and beautiful person so please don't ever think that what I did was in any way your fault. If you can find it anywhere in your heart to forgive me please do so...if there is anything I can do to help you please just let me know and I will do my best.

Your Brother, With much love,

Collin

I was extremely grateful to have my brother back in my life. Although he had hurt me in a way that will never be erased from my mind and is something that I will have to deal with for the rest of my life, I had forgiven him. At this time in my life he was the only "real" family I had. I have no words to describe how I felt and how much I wanted Collin to be in my life.

However, things drastically changed after prom of my junior year in high school with Dean and Peggy. We fought more than ever before and I just did not feel like a true part of the family anymore. I was done with being a foster child. I was about to enter into my senior year of high school. I had just been named mascot. I was finally on the cheerleading squad and felt accepted at school for the first time in my life. I started working at Subway and within two months was named assistant manager.

    My boss and I connected on a level that I had never experienced before in my life. She was sexually abused by her father when she was a child as well. I finally had met someone who new how I was feeling and what it felt like. One day she mentioned that if I wanted to emancipate, she would support me. I thought it was a great idea. Not long before this conversation, my car had broken down on the street near our house. I went in to tell Dean and Peggy. That conversation did not go over well. Dean was mad and said that none of his foster children knew how to take care of anything. I was extremely hurt by that reaction, because I was a child who tried my best to follow all the rules and be a good kid. I was even known as a "goody-two-shoes" among the other foster children and kids at school. It was not a name I was happy about, so I was upset from that reaction. I grabbed the phone and went into my closet and called my boss Margie. We talked things out and I finally fell asleep with the phone in my hands in my closet. When the cops called at 4 a.m. and told us we had to move the car due to it being a safety hazard, Peggy came into my room to get me so I could help. When she opened the door and saw that I was not in my bed, her first reaction was to say that I had ran away. That was the last straw for me.

Here I was a kid who had gone through Hell and back, yet I never once thought about running away from anything. I always stayed the course and did my best in all situations thrown at me. The next day I called my caseworker Lou. She talked to my judge and confirmed that I would still receive a full ride to college if I emancipated out at the age of 18. So that night I wrote a letter to Dean and Peggy. A few weeks went by and then I knew it was time to give it to them. The letter explained everything. But yet again I was met with a hand and anger. Here is an e-mail about what happened. I wrote this e-mail not long after the incident that changed my senior year forever.

Hey, how are you? I am good; I have a lot to tell you. I am no longer living with Dean and Peggy as of September 3. I started working at Subway in May and got to really know my boss. She felt just like a real mom and I really enjoyed her family. They all wanted to be my family. Things with Dean and Peggy hadn't been good for a while. I wrote a letter to Dean and Peggy. Saturday morning he came into my room and said "there has been lots of tension between us" I said "yes, hang on." I then went to the car and grabbed the letter I had written. I came back in and gave it to him. He read the first paragraph, got up from the bed, lunged at me. He grabbed my neck and threw me across the room and I hit the bed, rolled off, hit the dresser, slipped on the hair dryer and hit the wall with my head. Peggy came running down the hall and asked what was going on. I said 'I'm moving out when I turn 18.' She said 'you aren't going anywhere.' Dean grabbed me by the arm and threw me into the living room onto the couch. He said, 'it's not about your wants, needs or feelings; it's about all of ours.' I said, 'that's where you're wrong, because it is about me.' He asked why I hadn't come to them first. I said because I knew you would do what you just did. He said, 'then just leave right now.' I took off and went to the car. He ran after me and said, 'you can't have the f*cking car.' I told him I didn't want the car. I just wanted to grab my checkbook, paychecks and that I had worked my butt off for them. I then took off running down the street. It was a steep hill and how I made it to the bottom without tripping I'm not sure. The judge's wife saw me and picked me up. She didn't want me to say what had been going on so that if things went to court her husband could be my judge. I told her to take me to the Fina. That is where Margie was working. I walked and the owner of the Fina station looked at me once and both her and Margie said he hit you didn't he. The cops were then called and they came and picked me up to take me to the station to give them a statement. I had to do it ASAP knowing that Dean would be calling to report me as a runaway. The cops called my caseworker and they sent me to *my family advocator and I was put on respite until the 12th of September. I was then able to move in with my boss.*

It wasn't until my freshman spring semester in college when this actually made it to court. The rest of my senior year was set to this tone. I was finally free to be me and not another foster child. I was one of the very few foster children that went to this public school. I then got to finish out my senior year and be one of the first foster children to graduate with honors. Not only that, but for the first time in my life I would walk across the stage and be the first child that my biological mother would get to see graduate. I had found my birth mom in December of my senior year in high school!

Foster care was rough for me, but it made me who I am today. Not everyone who is in the foster care system has a story like mine. Other people look at children who are in foster care as bad people. In reality most of them are just from a bad situation. What the system needs is people caring for the children who actually care about the person, not the kind of money they can get. I thought the family I was with had my best interest at heart. But looking back I can honestly say I don't think they did. When I was 12 they asked me if I wanted to find my mother, and I said that I did. They "looked" for a few months but said they were not able to find her. I honestly don't think they ever looked. At the age of 14 I was told that no one would want to adopt a child that old; I was damaged goods. I thought of myself as that for a very long time. There are still days today that I actually still think that. I however now know that is not true. I am a princess to the King of Kings.

Chapter 4-Finding My Mom

John 1:12 -

But to all who believed him and accepted him, he gave the right to become children of God.

From the time I was about 12 until almost 18 I wanted to find my mom. My foster family that I lived with last told me that if I wanted to find my mom then they would look for her. A few months went by and finally were told that they could not find her. I shook it off and kind of just moved on. I really didn't put much thought into it until one day at work. I was working at Subway during my senior year in high school. One of my coworkers (Victoria) asked me if I wanted to find my mom. I said, 'yes, I do actually, but my foster family said they searched for her and couldn't find her, so I'm not really sure how I would go about finding her.' Victoria then asked if I had my birth certificate that had my mom's name on it. I said, 'yes I do, but I have had people look for me already and so far no one has been able to find her.' Victoria then told me to just let her try and see what happens. So I gave her my things the next day. I forgot about her looking for my mom. About two weeks went by and I still hadn't heard anything. One day I was at the store (Subway) and as I was walking into the office, Maggie was on the phone. As I started to open the door, she stopped talking and locked the door. I thought it was weird because there was never a moment where we had secrets between us until now. I just shook it off and went about my business. After we got home, Victoria stopped by the house and I knew immediately why she was there. They sat me down and explained that Victoria had received a response to an e-mail and Maggie just wanted to make sure it was true. I was in complete shock that it actually happened. I found my mom! December 9, 2005 was a day that would change my life forever.

Here is the email that was sent to my mom from Victoria:

Jane,

My name is Victoria, and I come from a small town out in Texas. I went to school with a girl named Janet for a few years, we now work together... She's asked me to look for her birth mother, because she is out of state care now. If you did not give a girl up for adoption, you may discard this mail now, and if you did and you aren't interested in contacting her, you should as well I suppose. We got your name off her birth certificate, and her father's name is Rodger Harald Jagger... If you are interested in being some part of her life I want you to know she's quite ready at this point... I'd appreciate hearing back from you. If you aren't the woman we're so desperately looking for, I'd also appreciate it if you'd mail me back saying so. Thank you for your time.

    About 9 hours later there was a response.

    Victoria,

Yes, I am Janet's mother! I've so badly wanted to find her for so long but had no idea where to look. Please let her know this and my contact info is below—she can contact me by e-mail, phone-collect if necessary. Oh my gosh, this is an answer to prayer!!!

    Little did I know that the phone call Maggie was making was to my mother double-checking we had the right woman. It took me two hours to make a response, because I was in complete shock. But what my mother did not know was that Collin called me this day out of the blue. I told him that I found mom and he called her and talked to her till 2 a.m. and then called me! This news made me feel like I could finally be a normal person. I was now going to be able to get some information on who I was, why I was in foster care, who my parents were and more family history. Little did I know that not only did I find my mom that day, but I also found my oldest and youngest sisters and my youngest brother. My middle brother had still not been found yet. I was not sure what I wanted to say to my mom, because to be honest, I did not think we would ever find her. So I had Maggie e-mail her for me. It read:

Jane,

It's Maggie that called you today about Janet. Well this afternoon when we got home, our friend that

found you came over and we set Janet down and told her about what we had done about finding you and she was very excited and is overwhelmed. She is the type of person that has to think things through and figure out what she wants to say and ask. She is a very cautious about her life and doesn't like to make rash decisions without praying or talking or writing them first. So it might take her a few days to call but she will and you can e-mail if you would like. Hope you're not disappointed that she didn't call. She's ok taking this all in. Talk to you soon,
Maggie

It's hard to describe what I was feeling at the moment. I had so many questions to ask. I wanted to know how many brother and sisters I had. What my heritage was, medical history and anything else she was willing to tell me. Below are a couple of the e-mails that were sent to me during the first three days of finding my mom.

From Jane:

Hi Honey. I don't know what to say! I'm thrilled that your friends have found me and that you and Collin want a relationship with me. I've been in tears off and on all day. Happy tears!

I want you to know that it's okay. You call me and/or e-mail me whenever you are ready to. I'm not going anywhere! I need to tell you that I LOVE YOU!! I have always loved you, Jan-Jan. I always will and there is nothing you or anyone else could do that would change that. You all have never been far from my thoughts and my prayer for years has been that you all would come back into my life.

I lived in Lawton, OK until early 1992, then moved to Oklahoma City, OK with my husband, Robbie. From there we ended up in Georgia with his mom and stepfather until they convinced him that he didn't need me and he filed for divorce. I moved back to Oklahoma City, OK and found out that you all had been adopted. I could never get anymore information. In Feb. of 1994 I met Stanley and on Feb. 18, 1995, we were married and have been married ever since. You have a little brother named Jordan who is 9 years old. He is in the third grade and loves school. He is also very excited to know that his big sister had found us and can't wait to talk to you. You also have a baby sister, Christy, who is 3 ½ years old. She reminds me of you a lot! You also have another brother, Stefan, who is 13. I still don't know where he is because Robbie refused me custody when we divorced. I haven't seen him in 12 years.

Your sister Amy is 23 (she will be 24 later this month). She is in the Army and is currently deployed to Iraq. She found me in June of 2003 and we got to see her for the first time at Christmas of 2003 when she came to Italy to spend Christmas with us. I sent her an e-mail this afternoon after I talked to Maggie to let her know that you had found me and that hopefully I'd be talking to you sometime soon. She is so excited to know this, she can hardly wait to come home to the U.S. and see you! At the time she didn't know that Collin would be calling me- how could she? I didn't even know!!

Speaking of Collin, he called me tonight and we spent a little over two hours on the phone. It felt so good to talk to one of my children! I wish I could hop on the next plane and come see you both. Someone pinch me please!

Honey, we have so much to catch up on, but know that I'm very proud of you and I wish I could have been there for you. If I had only known how things were for you two Stanley and I would have done everything in our power to get you home.

I love you!
(Sent Dec. 10, 2005 at 2:23 AM)

    My Dearest Janet,

Getting your e-mail last night was wonderful! I'm soooo happy that the two of you have found me; I'm sill pinching myself to make sure it's real! I know you have a ton of questions and I'm going to do my best to answer each one.

Where did you get your blue eyes from? That's an easy one to answer – those came from your Dad's side of the family. He had beautiful blue eyes.

Were you named after any other relatives other your middle name after me? Yes, the middle name is not only after me but it is a family middle name that has been passed down since at least your Great-Great-Grandma. Your first name is also mine. Janet is a form of Jane. It means "beautiful gift of/from God." Amy's middle name is also a form of Jane and so is Christy's. All of my girls have a form of my name as their name.

Our family is Irish, Black Irish, English and Indian.

Collin told me that after you two were adopted you were both abused. It broke my heart to hear it because I'd hoped that with it being a preacher and his wife that you all would at least be loved and cared for. I'm soooo sorry and if I had had any idea of what had happened I'd have done everything in my power to get you two back.

You and Collin (and Amy too) were taken from me one night when I had gone to a friend's home to work on Vacation Bible School stuff and my grandmother was watching you. Amy got it in her head that I had gone looking for your father and talked Collin into going with her to find me. They ended up at a convenience store and the person who was working there called the police. They took Collin and Amy to the house, didn't find me there, but found you and your great-grandmother and because we had roaches they took you guys to the shelter. I went to court the next day to find out what was going on and was told what I needed to do. I went home and did it and three days later went back to court where the judge asked the state why they removed you from our home. Their answer was that I had left you guys in the care of an elderly woman and that there were roaches in the house. The judge looked at them and told them that had just described 80 percent of the homes in Comanche County and they'd have to have a better reason than that. After sputtering and stammering around a bit they still couldn't come up with a better reason for you all to be kept out of my care and the judge told them that they had to release you guys to my custody by the end of the day. After that we constantly had a case worker looking over our shoulder and after Amy went on a court-ordered visit to Florida to see her dad, I came down with a pretty strong stomach virus. Our caseworker had told me once that if I ever needed help to call him and he would get me some help. I believed he was a good guy so I called him (at this point I had no back-up because my grandmother had to go New York to live with my aunt because I just couldn't take care of you two and her health needs – she was diabetic and was now having seizures with it and I just couldn't do it anymore). His way of helping was to come to the house the next day with the police and he took you two away to the shelter. I was furious! The caseworker had lied to me about the kind of help he would give me and I never saw it coming. I proceeded to go to court every six months as scheduled. Each time I would have a laundry list of things that the state said I needed to do to bring you guys home. I did them, went to court and instead of bringing you two home I was given another laundry list of things to do. This went on for at least two years if not longer. I re-married and once Robbie moved me away from Lawton he wouldn't le me come back to fight for custody of you kids. The state told Collin they didn't know where I was but they could have easily found me, my mom always knew where I was and she would have contacted me or given them the information to contact me. My being gone was the easy way for them to accomplish what they were about – back then, their big thing was removing children from decent homes (low income but decent otherwise), putting the parent through the wringer and then terminating their parental rights and getting the kids adopted. As a single parent who was trying her best, I was seen by them as not being good enough to have children. I never abused you kids in any way except by smothering you with love. I'm sooooo sorry that you have had to go through this and that your life was so hard. I would have done anything to change it.

I don't know where your father is or whether he is even still living. We were married November 17,1986 and in the summer of 1987 he decided that he really didn't want to be married to me even though I was pregnant with his child. He was there at the hospital the night you were born but when it came time for me to go the delivery room he opted to wait in the waiting room so my cousin Debbie went into the delivery room to help me. I believe with all my heart that he loved you but he just didn't know how to show it. At one point after you were born he had a tooth removed and the dentist put in a titanium screw to attach a false tooth to, they gave him morphine for the pain and he ended up hooked on morphine and from there got involved with other drugs. Never in front of me – he knew I couldn't stand them. He eventually went AWOL from the army, we didn't see him for several months and when he came back, he was hiding from the authorities still and when he felt they were closing in on him he disappeared again and I never saw nor heard from him again. I have heard rumors that he has died but I have nothing to confirm it.

I was not sure how to take all of this news. I was really excited I was finally getting answers to a lot of questions I have had growing up as a little kid. I now knew where I got my eyes from, my name from, and what my heritage was. As a foster child, these are all things that for some go unanswered their whole life. And for me I am now a senior in high school getting the opportunity to share who I was with all my classmates, things they new about themselves and each other since they were little. However that was not all the news I was going to get that day. The day I found my mom, I also got to find my older sister! Here is the first of the e-mails from her.

Janet,

WOW...I am not sure where to begin. I have waited for this day since my Dad took me from the two of you and Mom in 1989. I have never felt like a complete person b/c I was missing a big part of my life, a brother and a sister. You guys have always been in my thoughts and I have always wanted to find you.

Well....in 1989 my Dad was given full custody of me, he came and got me from Oklahoma and I moved to Jacksonville, Florida. When I got there, I already had two sisters and *a brother from my Dad's wife, her name is Becky. She is a VERY good woman, one of my best friends; she cared for me like I was her own. I grew up with Sam, Elle and Dusty. Sam is 22 yrs. old, married to James and has two boys, Callen and Coby, and they live in MacClenny, Florida. Elle is 21 yrs. old and she lives with Becky in MacClenny and is a massage therapist. Dusty turned 19 yrs. old this past October; he is living with Sam and working with her husband James. He graduated from high school last year. I am very close to them, especially since I have been in the Army, being away has actually brought me closer to them.*

I graduated with the class of 2000. I enlisted in the Army and left for boot camp August 6, 2000. I went to boot camp at Fort Leonardwood, Missouri. I then did my job training at Fort Jackson, South Carolina. My first duty assignment was Seoul, South Korea. I was there for two years...it was awesome, I love traveling the world. From there I went to Fort Belvoir, Virginia. I was only there for three months when I got selected to work at the Pentagon for the Chief of Staff of the Army. I worked there for 1 1/2 yrs.

In high school I ran cross country and I was a varsity cheerleader. My grades were ok...average...why do you think I joined the Army?? LOL :-)

I LOVE college football, I am a huge Florida Gator fan and when it comes to NFL I am a Tampa Bay Bucs fan. :-)

How did I find Mom....well, when I was in Virginia at Fort Belvoir I went online and used www.ussearch.com I provided them with the info I had of her and they were going to do what they could from that. About a week after I submitted my information I got an e-mail with all Mom's info....only problem was, she was overseas and I wasn't sure where or how to get ahold of her. So, when I typed her new name into a search engine on the computer, a link to the high school she attended in Lawton, OK popped up, so, I clicked on it. Apparently mom went to her high school reunion and they posted her e-mail address and her new name on the website.....so, I e-mailed her. She quickly responded and that was it really....I found her in June of 2003. That year I spent Christmas in

Italy with Mom, Stanley, Jordan and Christy. It was a dream....I was so happy.

I have since seen them a few more times, but with me moving around so much and deploying, I haven't seen them in over a year now. We are always talking on e-mail and when I can I call.

I am going to attach some pictures for you guys....I hope to hear from you both very soon. I know this e-mail was long and full of info, I am just so excited.

I can't wait to see you....

ALL MY LOVE, YOUR BIG SIS, Amy

Hey Amy,

Thanks for the e-mail, I was delighted to hear from you, I can't wait to meet you. I still can't really believe that I found you and mom, it's so exciting! I know that Collin is too. I am the mascot for my high school; I go to Goldthwaite High School. We are the Eagles. I have lived in many different homes over the years. It's amazing to be able to share my family history with my classmates now. They have been asking me for the past six years about my real parents and now I can answer their questions. Everyone says how much you and me look alike. I have very curly hair as well as you and the first thing everyone has pointed out is our nose. They say that it's definitely genetic. I enjoyed looking at your pics and reading your info. I have lots of questions but don't really know where to start, so I'll think about it some more and I'll e-mail you again later. Love, your little sis

I never knew I had an older sister, so I wasn't hoping or expecting to find her when I found my mother. It had been such a surprise to me. I couldn't believe that I no longer just had my older brother, but I had five brothers and sisters all together. To this day it is hard to believe there are so many of us.

I sometimes wonder what it would be like if we had all grown up together. Would we be close, would we hate each other? How different would our lives have turned out? Although I wonder those things, I know it was not part of God's plan for us to live together. I'm just glad that we have at least all found each other.

Chapter 5-Finding My Dad

Psalm 68:5-6 -

Father to the fatherless, defender of widows-

this is God, whose dwelling is holy.

God places the lonely in families;

He sets the prisoners free and gives them joy.

But He makes the rebellious live in a sun-scorched

land.

So it's summer of 2012. I am about a month away from graduating with my master's degree! Life is going great – I just got back from a study abroad trip to Fiji and New Zealand, one of the best trips in my entire life. One day I am interning in the offices at school; this office is run by four of the best cheerleaders during my collegiate years of my life. One day I'm in the office learning how to run a few different databases and the purposes they have. One of the ladies does a search of me to show how it brings up all of my addresses and my parents. When this happens I notice that my biological father is listed. I knew his name. In fact, I had done extensive searches for him after I found my mother, but nothing ever came up for him. I write down the information that is shown and just go on about my business, not thinking too much about it. A few days go by, and one night I'm sitting at home watching TV when I get the idea to do a google search on him to see what is brought up. Ironically, I have never thought about this before. So I googled him and a Facebook profile is brought up. I type out a message to him and before I could lose my nerve I hit send. This is what I said.

"Hi!

I know you have no clue who I am. You may not even want to know who I am. But I want/need to know something. I need to know if you are/were my father. If you want nothing to do with me then that's fine, I just need to know either way. I found my mom six years ago, and I have been looking for my father for a long time, almost 13 years. I know he may want nothing to do with me, that's why he left 24 years ago, but I need to know if you are him, and if you want contact. If you don't, then I will never contact you again, but will you please let me know either way.

If you have no idea who i am talking about then please let me know that as well, I am searching for my father, he left me and my mom almost 24 years ago, he served in the army. He has the same name as you, and lives in Oregon. I know all of this because it's on my birth certificate, not to mention there aren't that many people with that last name. He was married to a woman by the name of Jessica.

Please just help me find some answers or just close a chapter in my life. Thanks,

Janet Louise"

This was sent on July 8, 2012. 45 minutes later I got a response. I was very scared to open up that message on Facebook... but I did, and this is what he said.

> "Yes I am your father. I will try to answer your questions as best I can. I am shocked and happy you found me."

So for the next few hours/days we talked back and forth and this is what he told me.

Me: I am just as shocked as you are...I have no where to even begin

So what happened? Why did u leave?

Him: I would like to chat with you and just have a convo. Unless you hold against my past?

Me: Right now I'm all ears, I will give u the same respect I gave my mom

Him: My typing is slow. I had several issues when I left. I have completely changed from then

Me: What kind of issues?

I have had plenty of issues in my life; it hasn't been a real pretty one

Him: Mostly with your mom and I had issues

I have been in several VA hospitals for long periods

I was injured pretty bad

Me: How were you hurt?

Him: Helicopter went down I lost 85% hearing and my vision

Me: How long ago was this?

Haha I'm sorry, I'm very interested, I wanna know everything, it will help me so much

Him: 1993

HAHa? Ok

Me: Well I'll tell you a little bit about me, I am about a month away from earning my masters, I got my bachelors in communications, advertising and PR

Graduated high school with honors

Him: Ok, it is almost midnight here I will be back in morning I will get u some pics if you want ok

Me: That would be awesome. I have plenty on my page feel free to look at them!

Have a good night and I will talk to you tomorrow

Ok good night

Me: I'm sorry if it made it seem like I was laughing at your injuries last night, I didn't mean it like that, I was laughing at myself for bombarding u with questions

Him: It's ok I understand you have many questions. I am trying to upload some pics but my smart phone is being a pain

Me: So how's ur day?

Him: My day is going really good thanks. I am very excited you found me.

How are you? I am impressed at your education wow awesome

I hope you continue doing well

Me: I'm completely in shock, I can't believe I found you and u want contact

Him: Yes I have an interest in your life and would like it to grow from here.

Me: I just wanted to let u know I just want to take things slow

So for the next two days that is how my life was. It revolved around always checking my Facebook to see If I had any news. It also meant I now had a few decisions to make. This was going to change my life yet again. I needed to tell my mom that I found my father. I also needed to tell my step/adopted dad that I had found my biological father. I knew this would hurt him, yet he would be excited for me. I needed to make a decision on what kind of role I wanted now. But instead of making a decision right then, I waited and tried to gather more information.

Him: So a little about me, I am 49 and a disabled vet. I am not married at this time. I have a service dog. I have seizures and ptsd. I have to ask, are you mad at me? If you are I understand.

Me: No, I got all that out when I found my mom, I just want to know why you left, did you ever have any more kids.

Him: Me and your mom had issues that I didn't see as fixable. It was at the time my best option. Hindsight now well, I'm sure, I can't undo anything now. No other kids.

Me: So what about me? Did you know/care want anything to do with me?

Him: I didn't know about you, and I want to know as much as you care to let me.

Him: Wow thank you! I have missed so much, I don't want to miss anymore. I hope you are as happy as me right NOW! Thank you so much!! I am sorry to have made a decision that has hurt you.

Me: I'm pretty happy, it's crazy for me though. Just have to ask you though, did you ever go AWOL?

Him: No, I have honorable discharges.

Me: Where were you the night I was born?

Him: I was working at the pentagon and was overseas is all I can say. It was a top secret thing, I was a combat photographer.

Me: Where did your helicopter go down.

Him: It was top secret.

Him: Where did you get your last name?

Me: My stepdad adopted me 4 years ago.

Him: Ok, I take that he done well for you.

Me: He's a great guy. I've only known him for six years.

Him: I set up my Facebook profile as a joke and the joke was on me.

Me: Well I'm glad you did, otherwise I might not have contacted you.

Him: Your profile was the first one I ever really read and is a great inspiration to me.

Me: Have you ever heard of anyone allergic to onions?

Him: No, I'm allergic to fescue grass and raw tomatoes

Me: Mom is allergic to tomatoes too.

Him: I keep pinching myself this is real.

Me: Yeah, mom did that too after I found her. Did you ever get addicted to morphine?

Him: No

Me: do you have titanium screws in your mouth?

Him: No! My jaw was broken and wired shut to heal about 4 to 5 months.

Me: When did you leave?

Him: I was deployed March of 1987, so end of February 87. During that deployment I was reassigned to the pentagon and have not been to Oklahoma since.

Him: May I ask what inspired you to look for me?

Me: Well I have had an address for you in Harrisburg for six years. Every time I called I got hung up on. So I finally gave up. Friday I was interning and they were showing me something and then I got the nerve to google you yesterday.

The next day I got a call from my mom saying that my great grandmother had passed away. About a month or so goes by and I had received my stepdad's blessing to continue having a relationship with my biological dad. Mom wasn't too crazy about it, but she also supported me and said she was there if I needed anything. Rodger told me that I was allowed to say anything I wanted to him to help me heal. So one day he texted me and said he was not sure what to do. He had only known he had a daughter for about one month. I wasn't sure what I wanted from him yet. So this is what I told him.

Me: I don't mean to sound rude here because that's not what I'm trying to say. I am not really looking for a fatherly relationship from you. I have my stepdad and he's pretty awesome. I mainly wanted to know your side of the story and now that I know, my childhood can now be closed. I am not sure what there is for you to do.

Him: That's fine! What do you want from or with me? Ok well I'm not sure either? Now your childhood is over.

Me: The unknown of that chapter is closed. So many question were answered, and I can now move on.

Him: Now you know how to reach me. I will only reply and I won't bother you.

I wish I could have ended things good right here. But he decided not to keep going. Things were still very fresh for me. I thought that at the age of 49 he could have been a mature adult and deal with this adult-like, but that is not what happened. I know there were feelings that both parties had and neither one of us really knew what to do. I mean, who really could?

The same night, about one hour later, I received this.

Him: Glad your questions were answered, guess we are done.

Two hours after that:

Him: As long as your stepdad and mom are happy, why did you bother with trash like me anyway? Since they have last word I'm always gonna be a piece of shit. Thanks for the reminder, bye.

Yet again, two hrs after that:
Him: Hope you and your mom and father had a good laugh!!!! You're not different than Jessica. Thanks for the shithole reminders, just great.

The next morning I finally responded to him.
Me: I deserve a right to know why you left. It's not my fault you walked out. I have my whole life ahead of me and a lot of things going on in my life, but if you're going to act like this and judging from the texts you sent last night, then I don't want you in my life. I don't have time for drama.

When I first found my father I was so excited. Part of the reason I wasn't sure what I wanted from him is because once I got to see pictures of him, he was now a trigger. A trigger to something he knows nothing about. He looks like my boss's husband. I still to this day a year after I told him I don't want him in my life, don't know how to tell him that every time I look at him I see my boss's husband. I don't know if there will ever be a time in my life where I get the chance to rekindle this relationship with him. To be honest I am not sure I really want to either. Because you know what, although we don't have a relationship that is as close as it once was, I have the world's best father. I know that he would still move heaven and earth to help me. That father is not my biological father either. It is my stepfather Stanley. From the very beginning he has supported me, even when I hurt him and my mom.

They still took me back.

Chapter 6-Adult Adoption

James 1:27 - *Pure and genuine religion in the sight of God the Father means caring for orphans and widows in their distress and refusing to let the world corrupt you.*

It all started around Thanksgiving of 2007. I was now a sophomore in college. I was spending Thanksgiving with a family from church. I had found my mom and have yet to spend a holiday with her. At this point in my life though I had no access to my mother. We were not on speaking terms. You see after my high school graduation, I told her that I did not want to be in her life. I believe the exact words were: "you may be my mom birth, but Margie is my mom by choice." To this day, I regret saying that to her. I was hurt at the time and there were things going on that my mom Jane nor Margie knew were going on. But I also did not or could not say anything about what was going on. So I chose to take it out on my mom. Eighteen months later I was so alone and decided I wanted to mend things with my mom and stepdad. So I called my stepdad up and asked if I could come home for Christmas. I told him that I wanted to meet him and my little siblings, Jordan and Christy. I was told that he would get back to me in 24 hours. Well a little more than 24 hours went by and I just knew that I was not going to get my second chance. But God had other plans for me. Stanley called me later that next night and said I could come home. I had to tell them when I was coming and how long I was staying. So I set out to figure out a way to get home. I decided to finally ask the family I spent

Thanksgiving with to help me. They agreed and it was set that I would fly out for the whole winter break. That was a month. If things didn't work out then the family would help me get back home on the next plane. Well for three weeks I called my mom and asked what all I could do to get ready for this trip. The only thing I could truly remember and focus on was what my stepdad had written me about two years prior. This was the very first letter I had ever received that was handwritten from my stepdad (I believe it is actually the only letter I have that is handwritten!) He likes to type things out, so this letter is something I cherish to this day, eight years later.

Hey Janet,

It is much easier to type than it is to write a letter anymore.

I just wanted to take a minute to welcome you to our family. You can't imagine how awesome it was to find you after so many years. When Amy found us in 2003 I didn't know exactly how to handle her visiting us. But as soon as she came off the plane, there was an instant connection and when she started to call me dad, I was over-the-moon. So I had a better idea of what to expect when you came into our lives. Then we found out about your growing years and all of my uncertainty came back. "How is she going to handle having me in her life"?

Well I have gotta tell you, you couldn't have accepted me in a better way than you did. I still get weepy when you call me "Daddy." I know how difficult it must have been to extend your trust to me. I'm still blown away how easily you accepted me.

I know mom and dad can hardly wait to meet you, especially since I've been bragging on you. I can hardly wait either to finally give you a big hug and really welcome you.

I hope this helps you get through this period of waiting until May and your graduation.

Take care and may God bless you everyday.

With my love,

Daddy-o.

That letter got me through the waiting period of finally meeting the rest of my family. You see, none of them were able to come to my high school graduation. So until this point the only people I had ever met were my sister Amy, Mom and grandma.

I was extremely scared on how things were going to

go, but I had a peace in me knowing that God was going to take care of everything. Luckily I had written on MySpace what was going on during this trip. I have no other words on how to describe what happened during this trip. It has changed my life forever.

"This has been the best Christmas of my life. I have had so many good memories to keep. I started out after Thanksgiving, planning on coming to Ohio for Christmas to meet my mom and stepdad, brother and sister for the first time. I found my mom two years ago on the Internet and met her for the first time in May of 06 for my high school graduation. It wasn't a very good meeting. I hated her and didn't want to have anything to do with her. This past summer I started to talk to them again and decided I would come out and see them for Christmas. Well things happened and she

didn't follow through with what she said she would do. Packages that were supposedly mailed never showed up, and so on. Then in September, I received my records from the state of Texas about what why I was taken away and put in foster care. I asked her if what she had told me was the truth and she said yes. I then looked at them and saw that it was not what she had said. I decided not to contact her anymore. So the day after Thanksgiving I called my stepdad rick. i was thinking that since I had never meet him and stuff, I figured I owed that much. So I got the nerve to call him and ask if I could still come out for Christmas. I would bring the records and let them read them and see what the state's reasoning was. He called me the next day and said yes, I could come out there. As some of y'all know, I needed to borrow money from a credit card to make it out there. I asked everyone I knew. It came down to me asking my parents from church college group and them helping me. So for three weeks I planned and packed and called my mom and asked everything I could think of at the time on what to expect and got a general idea. Well it was nothing to how it turned out. I was pleasantly surprised. Not to mention I was flying for the first time in my life. I was double nervous. So anyway, I got off my final plane and was very nervous. I had to walk a long way before I got to my parents, so I had time to prepare myself for the last time lol. It was very nerve-wracking when I finally got there. I barely walked in when my mom came running up to me with my brother and sister in tow. My stepdad stayed back and just waited. I picked him out of the pack very easily. I walked up to him and my duffle bag broke. It was perfect timing because I no longer had to carry it.

Then I took two steps and my laptop bag broke as well. I went to the baggage claim and just waited until they said it was ready. My stepdad took one look at me and said you have that nose. We all have my mom's nose and so does all her family. We got my stuff and headed out to the house. I had to go to the bathroom as soon as we loaded up in the car and so we stopped. I was so hot that I got out of the car with just my shirt and Under Armor on, no jacket, and it was like 19 degrees when I got there. We ended up eating at a restaurant called Longhorn's, and that's when the bonding started. So anyways… .the next day was a little better. We went to church and I met everyone and was nervous. I still wasn't too sure on what to think of it all. I'm not sure if it was the second or third night that we finally sat down and talked after the kids went to bed; take that back, it was the second night. I called my sister and we kinda got into it and I got all upset. Well my dad was there to comfort me and tell me he loved me no matter what I chose to do. We sat down and talked about the records and it came with some pictures that were very hard to look at. And that's when I started to love my dad and my mom even more. He told me that if he knew where I was and what I was going through, then he would have moved heaven and earth so to speak to get me in their home and take care of me. At first I wasn't too sure how much he meant that, but every night since that night he has showed me in more ways than one. Days went by and we started to bond a little more. The time we had together without the kids was very cherishing. On Saturday we went out and shopped for mom, just the two of us. It was so much fun – we spent three hours together, laughing and just talking about our lives with each other. He has been the father that I have always wanted. It's been amazing. Well on Sunday, I met his extended family. His mom and dad loved me the minute they laid eyes on me, after all these years of hearing about me. I cried a lot to say the least. Then it came time for Christmas and stuff. Yesterday was the final moment that showed me everything I needed to know. I got upset about a specific incident and had said something as i was walking out the door to my grandparents, and then I came back in and apologized. My grandma took me in her arms and said, "it's ok honey, everyone makes mistakes and we are very glad you are back in the family where everyone wanted you for so long. Your father knows what it's like leaving the family and coming back in. He will tell you sometime and you will see – it's ok, we understand. We love you and want what's best for you." She made me cry even harder at that point and I just kind of looked at my dad and he knew I needed to know what she was talking about. We made the short car ride over to the house and got the kids and sent them to bed. At first, we just kind of sat there for a while. I was sitting on the floor by his chair, because I'm a little too big to sit in his lap, lol. He was playing with my hair and started to share with me what grandma was talking about. It made me cry and he tried so hard not to cry and was wiping my tears off my face. It was the perfect moment for a father and daughter moment. Mom went up to bed, and as I was going to bed I gave him the biggest hug of my life and told him thanks for sharing with me and he said, "whatever I can do to help it be easier on you I will do." It was very special moment in my life and that's when I knew for sure that he was my daddy no matter what our last names were, and if he could adopt me at this age then I'm sure he would. I'm just glad I'm getting the fairytale ending I have always wanted. I know I have said a lot about my me and my dad. Well, it's a girls dream to have a father in her life. Well I just got mine and I have my mom as well. They are so much alike on what they feel for me that no matter if it's my mom or dad, I have the family I have always wanted and it's a big one to say the least. I will have more on the rest of my two weeks here in Ohio later to come when I get back to Texas on the 11th of January."

I went back to school and did a lot of searching. I had to find out how to go about getting adopted and what the process was. On February 22, 2008, I was finally adopted by my stepdad. This is a moment in my life where, for the first time in many years, I felt accepted. The fact that his family was so accepting and encouraging to me meant the world to me. I was being shown what family really means. From this point on Stanley has been my father and always will be, no matter what.

Chapter 7 - College Graduation

2 Corinthians 3:3

And you show that you are a letter from Christ delivered by us, written not with ink but with the Spirit of the living God, not on tablets of stone but on tablets of human hearts.

December 11, 2010 and August 8, 2012 were two days that during high school I was told I would never make it to. The first one is my first college graduation. I received my bachelors in Communications with an emphasis is advertising and public relations. I have to admit there were days where I thought those teachers were right. My college years were some of the roughest years I had to face. I literally went from starting college with one of the greatest support systems in my life to being completely and utterly on my own within seven months. During those seven months I got one of the worst cases of mononucleosis. (I was told a week before I turned 19 that I might have lymphatic cancer because my lymph nodes on the right side were two inches wide and three inches long.) I was sexually molested for six months, sat on the witness stand for 2 ½ hours, was kicked out of the family over spring break. I failed one class first semester and was put on academic probation. I lost my job, quit one job and went back to doing what I did in high school. So yes, one could possibly say that graduating college was going to be a long-shot at best. Little did they know I had the big guy up stairs laying a path for my life.

I have to say though that during all this time, I had one person who was in my corner. We may live a nation apart, but it was during this year of 2006-2007 that our paths lined up and a bond was formed. I moved to college with a task of finding a girl named Wanda. Her aunt and uncle told me I should meet her, and that she should meet me. We were not given any more information other than names. So as I sit in my first college life group at church going around the room saying our names, she says her name, I say my name and we both look at each other and know that we need to meet. After church that day, our pastor took us out to lunch. As we headed back to the church, Wanda and I found out that we both drove the same cars, same color, make and model. We drove back to the dorms and we lived in the same building. As we were walking up, it was revealed we lived right next door to each other. It was such a good thing to know that. As the months went on, we got to be really close.

One night I finally told Wanda what was going on at home. My boss Margie's husband Kevin was sexually molesting me. It had been going on for about six months. He was a guy that was about 250 lbs, stocky, built and worked as a security guard at a state prison. He told me that if I told anybody, especially his wife, that all hell would break loose. Not only would his marriage fall apart, he would come to my dorm and kill me. When everything started he told me that he wanted me to be able to go to college and be able to have sex with guys if they wanted me to sleep with them. It was his idea to "help" me get over what my brother did to me. I was forced to do everything from oral sex to touching him inappropriately. He even tried to penetrate me several times and always failed.

It was in telling Wanda this that she finally opened up about something that had happened to her when she was five. Her cousin had molested her. She had never told anyone what had happened. Because I shared my story with her, she got the courage to finally tell her family. This was the start of a friendship that is unlike any other that I have. Wanda understands me in a way that no one else really can. We can be there for each other on our bad days, when triggers happen. We get it. Little did we know that Wanda's world was about to be turned upside down. When Margie finally found out what had been going on, I was kicked out of her family and was told to go get all of my stuff. Wanda went with me to get the last of my things.

On the way back to school, we were about to be in a huge rain storm, so we stopped at her aunt and uncle's house. This would turn out to be the last time Wanda would ever see her uncle. Two weeks later, he would be in a fatal car crash. Wanda and I have been through ups and downs together. The one thing that I know she gets me is by a poem she wrote for me when I graduated with my bachelors. One night Wanda and I were on the phone and I asked her to write a poem for me for my graduation gift. Literally five minutes after we hung up, this is what I had. The poem is word for word what I feel.

Behind Those Eyes

Sit for hours and gaze into her eyes

You will never perceive her

Interact with her till dawn

You will never discern her

Behind those eyes is a story

Full of heartbreak…pain… life

Pity, sympathy regret...she doesn't need that from you

She carries enough with her.

She won't tell of her story,

The pain shields behind insecurities and vulnerabilities.

Behind those eyes is a hope

A yearning for something better than she has seen

After all, she has seen in it all

She knows about losing, for it got her here

The hope to overcome fills missing pieces

She aches to be loved

Behind those eyes is a thirst

To know what love brings,

The undying, do anything for you, love

That kind of love is a stranger

Love to her has been disguised

Malice, misunderstanding, hate took its form

Behind those eyes is a girl who is learning

To be happy for herself

Her past is what has already happened,

Nothing to do with her future,

She is learning to trust herself

She won't let herself rely on another

Afraid the words will turn a person away

Behind those eyes is a love

A love so complex a stranger could not place it.

She talks, but watch what she does

Her actions speak the inner truths

A personal roadmap of where she's been

Behind those eyes is a woman who's learned independence

Looking further still lays the girl who craves life shared with another

Girl who has seen so much yet still wants to commit her heart

You don't know this girl, but you should.

You know the active, loud girl, not her shy quiet side

One day someone will witness the world she is hiding.

On that day those eyes will see someone worth the pain of past

Sit and talk to her for hours,

And still never discern her

Behind those eyes….she hides what matters most.

~Wanda.

All of this is what happened in my freshman year of college. My sophomore year, I reconnected with my family, got adopted and things changed for me. In April of that year, I was told to never step foot in the church I was attending because Dean and

Peggy's biological sons attended that church and were not happy that I told some of the members what had really happened. So up until September of 2009, I never attended church again unless it was with my family in Ohio.

In July of 2009, I was using the bathroom in the student center on campus. There were many flyers posted everywhere on campus advertising a girl's rugby team. Something inside of me told me to join this team. I knew nothing about the sport. That didn't matter. In August we met our coach. Josh told us from the very first meeting that he goes to church and attends a Bible study on Thursday nights. He extended the invitation every week stating that he would offer us a ride if we wanted to go. I refused to go for about a month. In September, I finally agreed to go. We met at a couple's house and they served us food. It was a coed study and they were starting a new series. We began a Matt Chandler study on the book of Philippians. I was intrigued from the very beginning. I came back every week, most of the time catching a ride with Josh. Then one night I was sitting in my dorm reading Romans 8:25-38. I did not understand what I was reading. So I sent Josh a text and asked him to explain it to me. He ended up calling me at 3 a.m. and we read the verses together and talked it out verse by verse. I began to ask Josh lots of questions about the Bible.

I will never forget the day of October 18, 2009. Just four days after I turned 22, I was sitting at a college function called engage. It was a program put on by the church every Sunday night. This night the pastor was telling us how he came to know the Lord. He talked about Romans 12 and Romans 8. At the end of the night there was an invitation offered if anyone wanted to come forward for prayer, questions or to make the Lord their savior. I wanted to but I was not sure if it was my time. As the music began, we all stood. I had tingling in my toes, all the way to the top of my head. I knew what I needed to do. I turned around and locked eyes with Josh, and then headed straight to our Bible study leader. We went to the corridor and I told him I was not saved and I needed to make Christ my Lord and Savior. He told me to pray. I said I did not know how to pray. But I had to pray this prayer myself. So I started to thank God for loving me enough to send His only Son to die on the cross. I was a sinner needing grace and that I wanted Christ to come live in my heart and save me. As we walked back to the group I was crying because for the first time I knew that I would be living eternally in Heaven. I still asked questions and about two weeks later. I finally made a public confession of an inward change and was baptized. I have lived a life that has been a light to others ever since.

Shortly after this time I went into an intense therapy session that was Christ-based. This is where I was shown that I was a princess. I was the daughter of the true high Priest. I was also showed where God was in all of my abuse. You see, although I was molested, the one place God was in that is that every time Collin or Kevin tried to penetrate they would not be able to.

You see, God was protecting me. It was 11 years after my first abuse that I was then showed where God was in the bad times. People ask me all the time how I could believe in a God who allowed me to go through such turmoil. I get it, I used to ask the same question. But you see, it was all so that one day I could share my story and be a witness for Him. Bad things do happen to good people, but this has been going on since the beginning of time when Eve ate of the apple and sinned against God. God then had to send His only Son to live a perfect life, die on a cross and then rise again three days later so that we can live with him eternally. But you see Christ is alive – He defeated death. All those things happened to me because God is going to use it for His glory. I don't know what kind of life I would have, but I know that I would not change anything if I could go back.

However, I am living proof that God is in the restoration business. It doesn't matter who you are, what you've done, or what has been done to you. God is willing and able to turn any tragedy into triumph.

"When you and I—like my brother—allow God to turn our mess into our message, He not only changes our lives, but He changes the lives of others too." --Micca Campbell

www.ingramcontent.com/pod-product-compliance
Lightning Source LLC
Chambersburg PA
CBHW051947160426
43198CB00013B/2331